The Postcard History Series

# East Central
# Georgia

## In Vintage Postcards

*Joeday*
*Merry Christmas 1999*
*Love*
*Barbara & Strick*

Freight Boat on the Oconee.

City Hall

Glimpse of Belview Av

Court House

Carnegie Library.

Greetings from
Dublin, Ga.

THE POSTCARD HISTORY SERIES

# East Central Georgia

## IN VINTAGE POSTCARDS

Gary L. Doster

ARCADIA

Published by Arcadia Publishing,
an imprint of Tempus Publishing, Inc.
2 Cumberland Street
Charleston, SC 29401

Printed in Great Britain.

Library of Congress Catalog Card Number applied for.

For all general information contact Arcadia Publishing at:
Telephone 843-853-2070
Fax 843-853-0044
E-Mail arcadia@charleston.net

For customer service and orders:
Toll-Free 1-888-313-BOOK

Visit us on the internet at http://www.arcadiaimages.com

*For Faye Thomas Doster*
*Who Has Made My Life Worth Living*

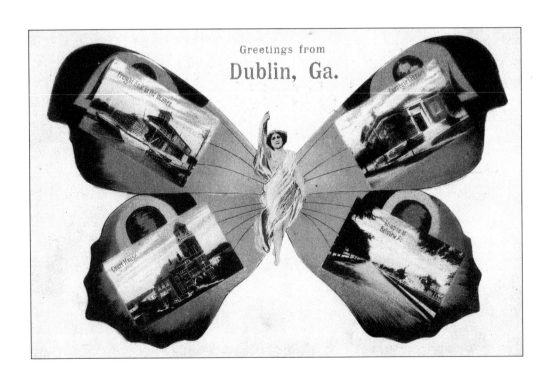

# CONTENTS

# ACKNOWLEDGMENTS

For help in various ways, including advice, information, and post cards, I wish to thank the following people:

Carl Anderson
Jim Dunn
Nell Dunn
Jerald Ledbetter
Ernest Malcom
Dan Marshall
Bill Moffat
Edwin Oldham
Hershel Reeves
Gordon Sanford
Bill Wheless

# INTRODUCTION

We are indeed fortunate that post cards* were invented and were so popular during the first several years of this century. In the clamor to satisfy the almost overwhelming demand for more and more post cards by the public, literally thousands of scenes were photographed that were never captured on film for any other reason. Over time, many of the homes, depots, court houses, stores, and other buildings so pictured have disappeared and these early post card views are the only images that remain. Two particularly interesting facts that were discovered while selecting and compiling the cards for these books concerned Georgia's Confederate monuments. A great many monuments were unveiled or dedicated on Confederate Memorial Day, April 26, and few of them remain on their original sites. The ladies of the United Daughters of the Confederacy and the old veterans themselves usually selected some prominent spot in the middle of town, almost always at the intersection of two main streets. Invariably, as automobile use increased over years, the monuments became traffic hazards and were moved to another part of town. Consequently, many of these post card views are the only pictures of them in their original locations.

Also of great interest are the views showing the intrusion of the automobile onto the scene. It is fun to note that the earlier post card views, those before 1907 or 1908, usually have horse- or mule-drawn wagons, buggies, or carriages in the street scenes (a few even show mule-powered streetcars!). Then, from that time to about 1912 or 1914, these views will typically show a mix of the animal-drawn vehicles and early automobiles. After this time, a wagon or buggy is only rarely seen, and the number of automobiles on the streets increased rapidly.

The collecting frenzy that swept the world began in Europe in the 1890s,

*Throughout the book, I have chosen to use the older spelling of the word, i.e. "post card" versus "postcard."

crept into this country before the turn of the century, and erupted a few years later. Many of the better quality post cards were produced in Europe, particularly Germany. Some of the post card factories in Germany were the size of cotton mills in this country, and they employed hundreds of people. For example, one German plant in 1909 had 112 cylinder printing presses and employed 1,500 workers. During the peak years of the post card collecting fad, more than a million people in Germany were employed in the post card business. In the three-year period from 1907 to 1909, more than 85,000 tons of post cards were imported into the United States from Germany.

In the Images of America book series published by Arcadia, the major effort has been to render pictorial books on individual towns or counties. And these are wonderful. Those of us who have an interest in preserving whatever we can of our past are hungry for books like this and they serve a valuable purpose. However, there are hundreds of smaller communities across every state that offer only a limited number of views of life of yesteryear that also are striking and important. Some medium-sized towns may have a handful of good views that show what their community and its people looked like nearly one hundred years ago. Many of the very small towns may have only one or two representative views. All of these are important, but none of them can support a book alone. Hence, this series of six volumes was conceived to provide a vehicle whereby a collection of early Georgia post cards from numerous small communities could be exhibited.

It is important to note here that this set of books is not intended to be any sort of scholarly work. It is merely an attempt to provide access to a selection of early views of Georgia that are not available in any other form, most of which have not been reprinted since their original publication. Many of the captions we provide in these books are no more than the caption printed on the cards when they were produced. Some additions have been made to some cards when the author had knowledge of some facts regarding the view in question. Other information came from the few reference books listed in the bibliography. To have researched each view and provided a comprehensive caption for each would have taken a lifetime of research, and then would still have been incomplete.

The author is a lifelong Georgian and has collected all manner of Georgiana for most of his life. Some of his other collecting interests are obsolete currency from the Colonial period through the War between the States, early letters and other documents, slave bills of sale and other items pertaining to slavery, Confederate letters and documents, old photographs, trade tokens, and Native-American relics.

# One
# AUGUSTA AND ENVIRONS

**AUGUSTA'S CONFEDERATE MONUMENT.** At 76 feet, the Confederate Monument in downtown Augusta is the tallest in the state. There were more than 10,000 people present for the dedication of the monument on October 31, 1879. A likeness of local Confederate hero Berry Benson stands atop the monument and the four corners of the base have statues of Confederate Generals R.E. Lee, T.R.R. Cobb, Stonewall Jackson, and Henry Walker.

THE EMPIRE LIFE INSURANCE BUILDING IN AUGUSTA.

THE SOUTH SIDE OF BROAD STREET IN AUGUSTA. This view shows a busy, industrious town.

THE MONUMENT IN AUGUSTA TO LYMAN HALL, BUTTON GWINNETT, AND GEORGE WALTON, GEORGIA SIGNERS OF THE DECLARATION OF INDEPENDENCE.

THE PATRICK WALSH MONUMENT IN AUGUSTA. This monument stands in Barrett Plaza in the square formed by the Union Station Railroad Depot and the Plaza Hotel.

FIRE DEPARTMENT HEADQUARTERS IN AUGUSTA.

THE CENTRAL AVENUE FIRE STATION IN AUGUSTA.

THE GEORGIA RAILROAD BANK BUILDING IN AUGUSTA.

THE YMCA BUILDING IN AUGUSTA.

**THE BIG FLOOD IN AUGUSTA, 1908.** The message reads: "Hello Helen—Have I not had a varied experience with water within the past two months. The storm at Wrightsville was bad enough, but the flood in Augusta was worse. Will write in a few days to Miss F. as I have a piece of news to tell. Angie."

**ANOTHER VIEW OF THE 1908 AUGUSTA FLOOD.**

AUGUSTA FIREMEN MANNING A HORSE-DRAWN FIRE WAGON IN FRONT OF THE FIRE
DEPARTMENT DURING THE FLOOD.

THE NATIONAL BISCUIT COMPANY BUILDING AT THE INTERSECTION OF SEVENTH AND
WALKER STREETS IN AUGUSTA. After the 1908 flood, the building looks more like it was hit by
a tornado.

Cotton Ginnery, Augusta, Ga.

A COTTON GIN IN AUGUSTA, C. 1912. This one looks like many of the gins in hundreds of other communities across the state at the time.

COTTON EXCHANGE, AUGUSTA, GA.

THE COTTON EXCHANGE IN AUGUSTA.

Old Union Depot, Augusta, Ga.

THE "OLD" UNION DEPOT IN AUGUSTA, C. 1912.

Union Depot from Tracks,
Augusta, Ga.

A VIEW OF THE "NEW" UNION DEPOT IN AUGUSTA.

Tubman High School, Augusta, Ga.

THE UNIQUE BELL TOWER OF TUBMAN
HIGH SCHOOL IN AUGUSTA.

ohn Milledge School, Augusta, Ga.

214319

THE JOHN MILLEDGE SCHOOL BUILDING IN AUGUSTA.

An Early Building of the Medical College of Georgia in Augusta.

The Paul Moss Orphanage
and Industrial Home,
Augusta, Ga.

This Orphanage Home was totally
destroyed by fire, Nov. 2, 1913.
WILL YOU HELP US?

The Paul Moss Orphanage and Industrial Home in Augusta. The home sported an impressive concert band. The printed message reads: "This Orphanage Home was totally destroyed by fire, Nov. 2, 1913. WILL YOU HELP US?"

THE AUGUSTA CITY HOSPITAL.

THE WILHENFORD CHILDREN'S HOSPITAL IN AUGUSTA.

LAMAR HOSPITAL IN AUGUSTA.

THE MARGARET HOSPITAL IN AUGUSTA. This view shows nurses standing on the second-story porch.

SACRED HEART CATHOLIC CHURCH IN AUGUSTA.

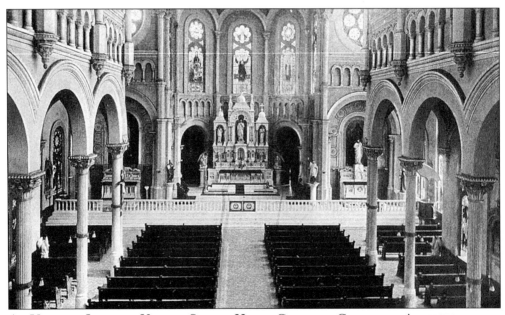

AN UNUSUAL INTERIOR VIEW OF SACRED HEART CATHOLIC CHURCH IN AUGUSTA.

ST. JOHN'S CHURCH IN AUGUSTA.

CHURCH OF THE GOOD SHEPHERD, THE HILL, AUGUSTA.

HOTEL GENESTA, ON THE CORNER OF JACKSON AND BROAD STREETS IN AUGUSTA.

THE DINING ROOM OF THE HOTEL GENESTA. The printed caption describes the hotel as "Elegantly Furnished. Every Modern Convenience. Open Year Round. Strictly European."

TEE NO. 1, COUNTRY CLUB GOLF LINKS IN AUGUSTA.

A SIDE VIEW OF THE AUGUSTA COUNTRY CLUB HOUSE.

THE HAMPTON TERRACE HOTEL. The castle-like hotel dominated the skyline, as shown in this pre-1907 view.

AN INTERIOR VIEW SHOWING THE ROTUNDA OF THE HAMPTON TERRACE IN AUGUSTA.

**THE PARTRIDGE INN, AUGUSTA.** Though not as large as Hampton Terrace, the Partridge Inn at Augusta was an impressive hotel. Printed information on the message side of the card advertised that the hotel had 125 rooms and 100 baths, an electric elevator, steam heat in all rooms, a 400-volume library available to guests, four polo fields, a telegraph office, a drug store, and numerous other amenities.

FOX HUNTERS READY TO START THE HUNT FROM THE PARTRIDGE INN IN AUGUSTA.

THE BOAT HOUSE AT LAKE VIEW PARK IN AUGUSTA.

BEECH SPRING AT LAKE VIEW PARK IN AUGUSTA.

**AUGUSTA MEMORIES.** The long, wooden covered bridge that spanned the Savannah River at Augusta and the huge stern-wheeler steamboats at dock evoke memories of another time.

**THE BUTT MEMORIAL BRIDGE AT AUGUSTA.** The bridge was named for Major Archie L. Butt, an aide to President Taft.

**DIVISION HEADQUARTERS OF CAMP HANCOCK AT AUGUSTA.** Camp Hancock was an important military facility during World War I. Its name was later changed to Fort Gordon.

THE YMCA BUILDING OF CAMP HANCOCK AT AUGUSTA, C. WORLD WAR I.

# Two
# BALDWIN, BLECKLEY, JASPER, PUTNAM, AND TWIGGS COUNTIES

South Wayne Street, MILLEDGEVILLE, Ga.

SOUTH WAYNE STREET IN MILLEDGEVILLE. A delivery wagon stands in front of Carr's Emporium, wholesale grocer. Next door is the City Cafe. A couple of doors farther down in the Aulmand Building is the American Telegraph and Commercial College.

City Hall.                    MILLEDGEVILLE, Ga.

CITY HALL AT MILLEDGEVILLE, C. 1912.

**STREET PEDDLING.** Shown here is a peddler with a donkey-powered, two-wheeled cart on the streets of Milledgeville about 1915.

**HANCOCK STREET IN MILLEDGEVILLE.** The card was sent to Demorest, and is postmarked July 11, 1913. The message reads: ". . . Had a nice bridge party today for Clara and went to the Hill Club this aft. I expected to go to Atlanta the first of next week, but I hear of a good many parties so don't know if I will get off. Lovingly M.H.H."

Court House, Milledgeville, Ga.

**THE BALDWIN COUNTY COURT HOUSE, MILLEDGEVILLE.** Completed in 1887, the building was remodeled and enlarged in 1937 and 1965, and continues in use.

**THE BALDWIN HOTEL IN MILLEDGEVILLE.** The hotel was located at the corner of Green and Wayne Streets. In 1910 the proprietor was Mrs. Emmie Jackson.

Masonic Building.    MILLEDGEVILLE, Ga.

**THE MASONIC BUILDING FRONTING ON HANCOCK STREET IN MILLEDGEVILLE.** Two doors down at 106 Hancock is Horne-Andrews Commission Company, cotton factors and wholesale grocers.

Male Building, State Prison Farm.    MILLEDGEVILLE, Ga.

**THE STATE PRISON FARM, MILLEDGEVILLE.** This post card showing the main building of the State Prison Farm at Milledgeville is postmarked March 31, 1914.

State Reformatory, MILLEDGEVILLE, Ga.

THE STATE REFORMATORY AT MILLEDGEVILLE.

Georgia Military College.
MILLEDGEVILLE, Ga.

**THE OLD CAPITOL.** Milledgeville was the capitol of Georgia from 1804 to 1867. After the state government was moved to Atlanta, the buildings were converted to the Georgia Military College. Here, cadets stand at attention in front of the old capitol building.

**THE BARRACKS OF THE GEORGIA MILITARY COLLEGE IN MILLEDGEVILLE.**

THE CENTER BUILDING OF THE GEORGIA STATE SANITARIUM IN MILLEDGEVILLE.

THE MALE CONVALESCENT BUILDING OF THE GEORGIA STATE SANITARIUM IN MILLEDGEVILLE.

THE GEORGIA NORMAL AND INDUSTRIAL COLLEGE IN MILLEDGEVILLE.

THE OLD GOVERNOR'S MANSION, MILLEDGEVILLE. When the capitol of Georgia was located in Milledgeville these buildings served as the Governor's Mansion and an annex to the capitol. At the time of this c. 1912 view, these buildings were part of the Georgia Normal and Industrial College in Milledgeville.

CHAPPELL HALL AT THE GEORGIA NORMAL AND INDUSTRIAL COLLEGE IN MILLEDGEVILLE.

A WIDER VIEW OF THE BUILDINGS ON THE GROUNDS OF THE GEORGIA NORMAL AND INDUSTRIAL COLLEGE IN MILLEDGEVILLE.

Atkinson Hall, Georgia Normal and Industrial College.   MILLEDGEVILLE, Ga.

*P.S. I cut the stone for this building several years ago—also the Lamar Hall—you have the rest of it—*

**ATKINSON HALL, THE GEORGIA NORMAL AND INDUSTRIAL COLLEGE IN MILLEDGEVILLE.**
The card was postmarked April 6, 1910, and was mailed to Confluence, Pennsylvania. The message reads in part: "I am here yet. I haven't finished my work. Am waiting on materials. E.P.L. P.S. I cut the stone for this building several years ago—also the Lamar Hall. You have the rest of it."

Terrell Hall, Georgia Normal and Industrial College.   Milledgeville, Ga.

**TERRELL HALL OF THE GEORGIA NORMAL AND INDUSTRIAL COLLEGE IN MILLEDGEVILLE.**

THE COUNCIL CHAMBER AND WATER TOWER IN COCHRAN, C. 1909.

THE CONFEDERATE MONUMENT IN COCHRAN. The monument was unveiled on Confederate Memorial Day, April 26, 1910, at the intersection of Second and Beech Streets. As with many other monuments that were placed in the middle of streets, increased traffic in years to come required their removal to a less hazardous location. The Cochran monument was moved in 1935 to the old city school grounds.

THE PUBLIC SCHOOL IN COCHRAN IN 1909.

THE THORNLEY HOTEL ON SECOND STREET IN COCHRAN. In 1910 the hotel was operated by Mrs. Leslie Thornley and a room cost $2 per day.

THE FARMERS BANK OF MONTICELLO.

New County Court House,
Monticello, Ga.
Erected 1907.

THE JASPER COUNTY COURT HOUSE IN MONTICELLO. The courthouse was built in 1907 by J.W. Beeland at a cost of $44,400.

PART OF THE TOWN SQUARE IN MONTICELLO. The Furse Drug Company on the corner not only dispensed medicines, but, as the sign indicates, they were dealers for Southern Home Pure Lead and Zinc Paints.

THE CENTRAL RAILROAD DEPOT AT MONTICELLO WITH THE TRAIN STANDING AT THE STATION. The Central of Georgia was the only railroad that served Monticello.

A VIEW OF THE SOUTH SIDE OF THE TOWN SQUARE IN MONTICELLO. Shown here are the Jasper County Bank and Benton Supply Company Department Store with a concrete horse watering trough in the middle of the street.

THE MONTICELLO HOTEL. This post card of the Monticello Hotel was postmarked November 27, 1906. The hotel featured a second-story balcony where guests could overlook the town.

THE PRESBYTERIAN CHURCH IN MONTICELLO. The church was an impressive clapboard structure.

MAIN STREET IN SHADY DALE, 1911.

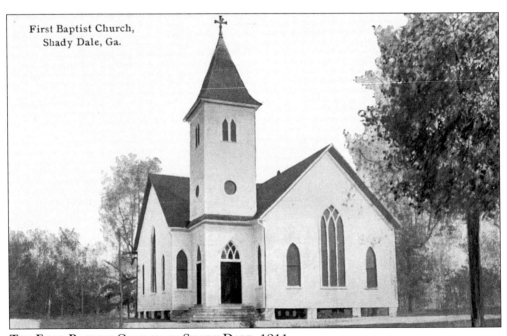

THE FIRST BAPTIST CHURCH IN SHADY DALE, 1911.

THE PUTNAM COUNTY COURTHOUSE, EATONTON. The original part of the Putnam County Courthouse in Eatonton was built in 1824. This post card was made soon after the building was remodeled and enlarged in 1905 by W.J. Beeland at a cost of $36,500.

MARION STREET LOOKING EAST IN EATONTON, C. 1907.

PRIVATE HOMES IN EATONTON IN 1909.

E.F. BRONSON'S HOME IN EATONTON.

MADISON AVENUE IN EATONTON, C. 1910.

WEST MARION STREET IN EATONTON.

A VIEW OF THE MIDDLE GEORGIA COTTON FACTORY IN OPERATION IN EATONTON.

THE TWIGGS HIGH SCHOOL IN JEFFERSONVILLE, C. 1910.

# *Three*
# Bulloch, Burke, Effingham, Jenkins, and Screven Counties

A Bird's-eye View of North Main Street in Statesboro, c. 1906. The large building on the corner in the center was the Statesboro Buggy & Wagon Company, dealers in vehicles, harness and leather goods, coffins and caskets, and horses and mules.

STATESBORO'S NORTH MAIN STREET AT GROUND LEVEL.

GEORGIA COTTON. This street scene in Statesboro, c. 1907, shows a street crowded with wagonloads of cotton, a familiar sight across much of Georgia at this time.

THE SIMMONS BUILDING. Located on South Main Street in Statesboro, this building housed Simmons Grocery and the Simmons General Merchandise Company.

THE BANK OF STATESBORO, SOUTH MAIN STREET.

Rountree Street, Looking South, Statesboro, Ga.

ROUNDTREE STREET IN STATESBORO, LOOKING SOUTH.

Looking East, Showing East Main St.
and Jaekel Hotel, Statesboro, Ga.

THE JAECKEL HOTEL IN STATESBORO. The caption printed on this view of East Main Street has the name Jaeckel Hotel misspelled. Mr. G. Jaeckel was the proprietor.

A View of Some Private Homes on Lewis Street in Statesboro, c. 1910.

Another c. 1910 View of Some Residences in Statesboro. Pictured here are homes on Kennedy Street.

A Real-Photo View of the Mansion of Mr. J.P. Williams in Statesboro in 1913.

A Fine c. 1910 View of a Hotel and the Collins Home in Statesboro.

The Boys' Dormitory at the First District State Agriculture College in Statesboro.

The Public School in Midville, 1912. This large brick building probably housed all grades of elementary and high school.

**THE BURKE COUNTY COURT HOUSE IN WAYNESBORO.** The courthouse was built in 1857 at a cost of $6,500. An addition was made in 1900 and an office annex was added in 1940. Restoration in recent times cost more than $1 million. The Confederate Monument was originally located in the local cemetery where it was dedicated on Confederate Memorial Day, April 26, 1878. It was moved to the intersection of Liberty and Peace Streets in 1899, but was moved back to the cemetery site in the early 1950s.

**MAIN STREET, WAYNESBORO.** This real-photo post card of the main street in Waynesboro, c. 1910, shows some fancy ladies passing in front of the business of Mr. Thomas Quinney, a cotton buyer and dealer in general merchandise.

**THE SCHOOL HOUSE IN WAYNESBORO.** It appears to be a somewhat dismal-looking place in this *c.* 1910 view.

**THE INTERIOR OF THE METHODIST CHURCH IN WAYNESBORO.** Its magnificent pipe organ can be seen here.

THE RESIDENCE OF MRS. INEZ W. JONES IN WAYNESBORO.

THE C.W. SKINNER'S RESIDENCE IN WAYNESBORO, C. 1912. Mr. Skinner was an undertaker and dealer in general merchandise.

The Guyton Pharmacy, Dr G. C. Guerard, Prop., Guyton, Ga.

DR. G.C. GUERARD'S PHARMACY AT GUYTON.

THE S.A.I. IN GUYTON. The entire student body must have been in attendance the day this photograph was made in 1908.

**THE EFFINGHAM COUNTY COURT HOUSE IN SPRINGFIELD.** The courthouse was completed in 1908 at a cost of about $40,000.

**SPRINGFIELD ACADEMY.** This was quite a large school for such a small community; in 1910, the population of Springfield was 300.

**MAIN STREET, SPRINGFIELD.** In this *c.* 1914 view, a wagon is parked outside J.B. Simmons' general merchandise store, next door to the drug store.

**LAUREL STREET LOOKING NORTH FROM BRINSON'S STORE IN SPRINGFIELD.** Brinson's Store was owned by George M. and R.R. Brinson.

THE JENKINS COUNTY COURT HOUSE IN MILLEN. Built in 1910, this courthouse was completed at a cost of $37,000. The Confederate Monument was placed erected June 3, 1909.

**THE UNION RAILROAD DEPOT IN MILLEN.** Mullen was served by the Central of Georgia Railway and the Mullen and Southwestern Railway.

A GRAND VIEW OF THE COTTON PLATFORM AND RAILROAD YARDS IN MILLEN, C. 1909.

**THE BANK OF MILLEN.** The cashier of the Bank of Millen in 1910 was C.E. Attaway.

A STATELY HOME IN MILLEN ABOUT 1912.

THE HOTEL ESTELL, MILLEN. The artist who prepared this drawing of the Hotel Estell in Millen added a lot of vehicles and an extra-wide street.

ROCKYFORD'S SOUTH MAIN STREET, LOOKING SOUTH FROM THE DEPOT, C. 1912.

THE OGEECHEE RIVER AND SWAMPLANDS. One of Rockyford's claims to fame was this 7/8-mile-long wooden bridge across the Ogeechee River and the swamp on each side. The sender, who was obviously a traveling salesman (or "drummer") wrote to New York, May 10, 1912: "Dear Mother, Have been out to Sylvania Ga again and stopped off here to call on the stores. I reached here 10 minutes past nine this morning. it took me just one hour to complete my work here and have got to hang around until four o'clock to get a train back to Savannah. It is good and hot today, lots of love Ross."

The Pfeiffer Hotel in Sylvania, early 1900s.

No Spitting in the Stove. An interior view of the Pfeiffer Hotel in Sylvania, with the guests gathered around the stove in the lobby. Apparently, management discouraged spitting on the stove by placing four cuspidors around it.

Court House Sylvania, Ga.

**THE COURT HOUSE IN SCREVEN COUNTY.** Built sometime around the turn of the century, it was the seventh courthouse built in the county after it was formed on December 14, 1793. The building is no longer extant.

Part of Public Square, Sylvania, Ga.

**PART OF THE PUBLIC SQUARE IN SYLVANIA, C. 1912.** The Confederate Monument in the center of the square was dedicated on Confederate Memorial Day, April 26, 1909. The monument was removed to the city park about 1950, when the square became a parking lot.

Screven County Oil Mill, Sylvania, Ga.

**THE SCREVEN COUNTY OIL MILL AT SYLVANIA.** This 1908 card showing the oil mill carries an interesting message. The writer was obviously an automobile salesman, writing to Don in North Kingsville, Ohio: "I am on the go all the time now. I am here placing a car and learning a man how to drive. He owns this oil mill. They make cotton seed oil. I will write you when I get back to Atlanta as I don't know how long I will be here. Hope you are having a good time this summer. I just wrote Ike a letter. Ed."

A LARGE CROWD GATHERED IN FRONT OF THE DRUG STORE IN THE HILTON BUILDING IN SYLVANIA IN 1907.

GOLOID SCHOOL IN SYLVANIA, C. 1908. Students of all ages gather in front of the one-room school.

# *Four*
# COLUMBIA, HANCOCK, McDUFFIE, AND WARREN COUNTIES

**DODGE PLACE, GROVETOWN.** The large, two-story frame structure pictured here is identified by the sender as Dodge Place, Grovetown, Georgia.

THE HIGH SCHOOL IN HARLEM, C. 1910.

THE METHODIST EPISCOPAL CHURCH, HARLEM. This real-photo post card showing the Methodist Episcopal Church in Harlem was mailed to Bloomington, Illinois. The sender wrote: "Have spent this week here and will be in Warrenton next week, so you can write us there. Have awful hot weather here. Tell Pa everyone here has a Jersey cow. Ella."

METHODIST CHURCH, CULVERTON, GA.

A c. 1906 VIEW OF THE METHODIST CHURCH AT CULVERTON.

Tenth District Agricultural School, Granite Hill, Ga.

THE TENTH DISTRICT AGRICULTURAL SCHOOL IN GRANITE HILL. The printed message on the card read as follows: "Superior advantages at a minimum cost for boys and girls of the Tenth Congressional District. Good buildings, strong faculty, healthy location. For information address, Granite Hill, Ga."

Dining Hall, Tenth District Agricultural School, Granite Hill, Ga.

A CLOSE-UP VIEW OF THE DINING HALL AT THE TENTH DISTRICT AGRICULTURAL SCHOOL IN GRANITE HILL.

Boys' Dormitory, Tenth District Agricultural School, Granite Hill, Ga.

A CLOSE-UP VIEW OF THE BOYS' DORMITORY AT THE TENTH DISTRICT AGRICULTURAL SCHOOL IN GRANITE HILL.

WILLOW DALE FARM AT MAYFIELD, "THE HOUSE OF THE BIG GUINEA PIGS."

THE CAMILLA-ZACK COUNTRY LIFE CENTER IN MAYFIELD. The community center was named for former slaves, Zacharias Hubert and his wife, Camilla Hillman Hubert, successful farmers in the community. It was begun in 1931 by one of their sons, Benjamin.

79

**THE COTTON TEXTILE MILL AT JEWELL, ON THE WEST SIDE OF THE OGEECHEE RIVER, 13 MILES EAST OF SPARTA.** The original mill was built of rock in the 1830s and it remained as the core of the building as it was enlarged over the years. Much of what is seen here was added in the 1870s and 1880s. The mill burned to the ground in 1927 and was not rebuilt. The town of Jewell was originally called Rock Factory, after the mill. The town was renamed Shivers after mill owner William Shivers. In 1856, Daniel A. Jewell bought the mill and the town became Jewell.

THE HANCOCK COUNTY COURT HOUSE IN SPARTA. The cornerstone was laid on Washington's birthday in 1882. The architects were Parker and Bruce, and the builder was James Smith.

THE DRUMMERS' HOTEL IN SPARTA. Built in 1851, the hotel provided a home away from home for salesmen and other travelers for many years. Originally called the Edwards House, its name was changed in 1896. It became the Lafayette Hotel in 1941 and operated until 1973. In recent years, the building was restored to provide housing for the elderly.

81

A Spectacular Real-Photo View of the Main Street of Sparta in 1907. The American flag flies over The Union Store, dealers in general merchandise.

A Close-up View of the Front of The Union Store in Sparta with a Sign Advertising Mitchell Wagons.

High School — Sparta, Ga.

**THE HIGH SCHOOL IN SPARTA, C. 1910.** Part of the sender's message reads: "Does this look natural. Miss Killebrew is going to teach in the front room in the Manual Training Building."

**THE MONTOUR MILL.** This huge four-story cotton mill in Sparta was the Montour Mill, built by George W. Watkins in 1852. It was one of the few brick buildings in town and stood in disrepair for many years before before finally being demolished in 1951.

THE PRESBYTERIAN CHURCH ON
BROAD STREET IN SPARTA, BUILT IN
1903.

THE METHODIST CHURCH AT THE CORNER OF HAMILTON AND BOLAND STREETS IN
SPARTA. When this post card view of the church was made in 1909, a printed message claimed
that the church was 101 years old. It burned down in 1910.

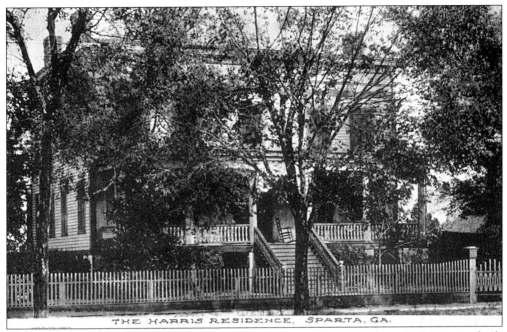

**THE HARRIS RESIDENCE, 720 ELM STREET.** The two-story Harris residence in Sparta was built *c.* 1845 and still stands.

THE THOMAS AND TURNER RESIDENCE IN SPARTA.

**THE G.W. RIVES RESIDENCE, SPARTA.** This post card was postmarked April 22, 1921, and has the following message: "You ought to be over here with us! We are having a fine time. Zoe is so good to us and gives us so many wonderful things to eat that we are getting fatter every day. Will be home Monday. Jack says hello. Love, Louise."

**THE OHLMAN RESIDENCE AT SPARTA.**

**THE MCDUFFIE COUNTY COURT HOUSE IN THOMSON.** The courthouse was completed in 1872 at a cost of $15,000. The building is still in use after undergoing extensive renovations and additions in 1934 and 1970.

STUDENTS OF THE PUBLIC SCHOOL AT THOMPSON IN 1910.

MAIN STREET, THOMSON. Although this card depicting the wide dirt main street through Thomson was produced c. 1910, it was not mailed until May 16, 1917. The sender wrote to Grand Rapids, Michigan: "Dear Clara: Just got here. We left Elberton at 6:00 this A.M. and rode 134 miles to this town. We leave here at 2:00 A.M. tonight and have to ride all night and part of tomorrow. We have to ride about 225 miles. We get awfully tired of riding and get sleepy too. Lots of love, Papa.

A GRAND VIEW OF DOWNTOWN THOMSON, C. 1908. Mule-drawn wagons congregated in the street. Note the stone watering trough in the street on the right.

**THE KNOX HOTEL.** The hotel was a center of activity in Thomson when this card was printed *c.* 1909.

**THE HOME OF THOMAS E. WATSON IN THOMSON.** Watson was a controversial politician around the turn of the century. He opposed allowing blacks to vote, and publicly denounced Jews and Catholics. Watson was elected to the Senate in 1920, but died in 1922 before his term was completed. Georgia Governor Thomas Hardwick appointed 87-year-old Rebecca Latimer Felton to temporarily take the office. Although Mrs. Felton served only one day, she holds the distinction of being the first female senator in the country.

**THOMSON HARDWARE.** On this post card of Thomson Hardware, mailed to Orlando, Florida, in 1909, the sender has penned the message, "This or no other place can touch Orlando."

First Baptist Church, Thomson, Ga.

18425

THE FIRST BAPTIST CHURCH IN THOMSON, C. 1915.

John E. Smith Manufacturing Co., Thomson, Ga.

Ga
7362

7362

Inside Dimensions
Length 36 Ft 0 In
Width 8' 6"
Height 7' 4"

THE JOHN E. SMITH MANUFACTURING COMPANY IN THOMSON. This company ran a cotton mill.

**THE MCGREGOR RESIDENCE.** The residence of Mr. L.D. McGregor, a lawyer in Warrenton, shows fancy trim typical of Southern homes built around the turn of the century.

**WARRENTON HIGH SCHOOL.** This pre-1907 view of Warrenton High School carries a message from one of the teachers: "My dear Ruth: I am sending picture of my place of business. The windows marked are in my room. The little porch is where my pupils march out. I tell you I have a long line of them. We have a very pretty brick building. You did not send me a picture of the school in Indiana. Please send me one. I hope you will write soon, you make your letters few and far between. Have you had spring fever yet? I'm just recovering. Lovingly, Emma."

# Five
# EMANUEL, JOHNSON, AND LAURENS COUNTIES

THE JAMES-CHEATHAM BLOCK IN ADRIAN, C. 1914. The Citizen's Bank can be seen on the corner.

**The Peddy Building in Adrian, c. 1914.** The business in the middle of the building had a sign listing some of their wares that were on sale, which included dry goods, notions, hats, caps, paints, suits, glass, crockery ware, shoes, and overalls.

**The Central of Georgia Railroad Depot in Adrian.** Adrian was also served by the Wadley and Mount Vernon Railroad.

THE BANK AND POST OFFICE BUILDING IN GRAYMONT, 1912.

GRAYMONT ACADEMY. The academy was an attractive building with a beautiful bell tower.

A STREET SCENE IN STILLMORE, C. 1912.

THE CANOOCHEE HOTEL IN STILLMORE. The hotel was owned by Nat Hughes. This card was mailed October 12, 1910, and carries the following message: "Dear Walter tell your mama to give you ten cents and let you go to the ten cent store and get me a jug that holds a gallon. I will be over to night. From Aunty W.A."

**THE HIGH SCHOOL BUILDING IN STILLMORE, C. 1908.** This building appears to have had more room than students.

**THE METHODIST EPISCOPAL CHURCH IN STILLMORE, C. 1911.**

**THE PEOPLE'S BANK IN SUMMIT, C. 1910.**
The bank's president at that time was J.A. Jones, who was also the town dentist, and the cashier was S.J. Flanders.

Citizens' Bank Building, Swainsboro, Ga.          Bell & Youmans, Publishers.

THE CITIZEN'S BANK IN SWAINSBORO, C. 1908.

**The Emanuel County Court House.**
This building in Swainsboro is no longer standing.

Court House, Swainsboro, Ga.

Swainsboro High School, Swainsboro, Ga.

The High School Building in Swainsboro, c. 1910.

Residence of Mrs. A. D. Coleman, Swainsboro, Ga.

THE RESIDENCE OF MR. A.D. COLEMAN IN SWAINSBORO, C. 1910.

Residence of J. L. Carmichael, Swainsboro, Ga.                    Bell & Youmans, Publishers.

THE CARMICHAEL RESIDENCE, SWAINSBORO. This post card view of the residence of Mr. J.D. Carmichael in Swainsboro was postmarked June 18, 1908.

**DEXTER, C. 1912.** This bird's-eye view of Dexter shows a large sprawling community.

THE MT. CARMEL BAPTIST CHURCH NEAR DEXTER.

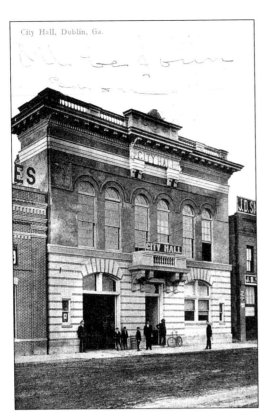

City Hall, Dublin, Ga.

**DUBLIN CITY HALL, C. 1908.** The large open doorway on the left was probably where the town's fire-fighting equipment was kept.

**THE LAURENS COUNTY COURT HOUSE IN DUBLIN.** The courthouse was built in 1895 and was used until 1962.

U. S. Post Office, Dublin, Ga.

THE U.S. POST OFFICE BUILDING IN DUBLIN, C. 1912.

Jackson St., looking East, Dublin, Ga.

JACKSON STREET, LOOKING EAST. This view of Dublin shows the courthouse in the distance. Robinson Hardware can be seen in the brick building on the corner on the right.

103

THE CORNER OF JACKSON AND JEFFERSON STREETS IN DUBLIN IN 1912. Hicks Drug Company was located on the corner; next door was Bailey and Folsom, dealers in clothing, hats, and furnishings.

JEFFERSON STREET, LOOKING NORTH, IN DUBLIN, 1908.

ANOTHER DUBLIN STREET SCENE, LOOKING NORTH FROM THE DEPOTS.

THE CORNER OF JACKSON AND JEFFERSON STREETS IN DUBLIN, LOOKING FROM COURT PARK.

First National Bank Building, Dublin. Ga.

THE FIRST NATIONAL BANK OF DUBLIN AT 47 WEST JACKSON STREET. In 1910, A.W. Garrett was the cashier.

AN UNUSUAL INTERIOR VIEW OF KNIGHTON AND FLANDERS' DRUG STORE IN DUBLIN, C. 1912.

THE JOHNSON STREET SCHOOL BUILDING
IN DUBLIN IN 1907.

Johnson Street School Building, Dublin, Ga.

Paul E. Trouche, publisher, Charleston, S. C. — Germany

RAILROAD JUNCTION. Three railroads served Dublin—the Central of Georgia; the Macon, Dublin, and Savannah; and the Wrightsville and Tennille.

Marcus Street, North, Wrightsville, Ga.

NORTH MARCUS STREET IN WRIGHTVILLE, C. 1910.

JOHNSON COUNTY COURT HOUSE, WRIGHTSVILLE, GA.

THE JOHNSON COUNTY COURT HOUSE. Built in Wrightsville in 1895, the courthouse was renovated in 1938. Golucke and Stewart designed the building, and it was built by Wagner and Gorenflo.

**WARTHEN COLLEGE IN WRIGHTSVILLE.** This card was mailed February 14, 1914, and the writer said: "Don't think I have forgotten you because I haven't written sooner. The other side of this card looks familiar, doesn't it. Zula."

**THE FIFTH AND SIXTH GRADES AT WARTHEN COLLEGE IN WRIGHTSVILLE IN 1908–1909.** All of the students names are recorded on the message side.

THE MUSIC CLASS AT WARTHEN COLLEGE IN WRIGHTSVILLE IN THE SPRING OF 1911. The students with numbers written on them are identified on the message side of the card.

THE SOPHOMORE CLASS AT WARTHEN COLLEGE IN WRIGHTSVILLE, C. 1911.

110

# *Six*
# JEFFERSON AND WASHINGTON COUNTIES

SMITH BROTHERS AND COMPANY, BARTOW. This 1911 advertising post card for Smith Brothers and Company claimed "We sell everything that men, women and children wear and eat."

Louisville Academy, Louisville, Ga.

**LOUISVILLE ACADEMY.** This *c.* 1910 post card view of Louisville Academy in Louisville has the date 1891 over one window, presumably the date the building was erected.

Broad Street, Louisville, Georgia.

BROAD STREET IN LOUISVILLE.

BUSINESS SECTION, Louisville, Ga.

A VIEW OF THE BUSINESS SECTION OF LOUISVILLE, C. 1910.

SLAVE MARKET, BUILT IN 1758, Louisville, Ga.

**THE SLAVE MARKET AT LOUISVILLE.** Built in 1758, the market still stands as a popular tourist attraction.

PRESBYTERIAN CHURCH, Louisville, Ga.

**THE STATELY PRESBYTERIAN CHURCH BUILDING IN LOUISVILLE, C. 1910.**

Holmes Drug Co., Corner Main and Railroad Sts., Wadley, Ga.

THE HOLMES DRUG COMPANY IN WADLEY. Located on the corner of Main and Railroad Streets, the company was owned by W.H. Holmes. A dry goods store operated by Mr. M. Steinberg was next door.

SCHOOL, Wadley, Ga.

THE PUBLIC SCHOOL AT WADLEY IN THE EARLY 1900S.

Depot, Wrens, Ga.

THE AUGUSTA SOUTHERN RAILROAD COMPANY. Wrens was served by the Augusta Southern Railroad Company, which ran from Augusta to Sandersville when it was formed in 1894.

THE WASHINGTON COUNTY COURT HOUSE IN SANDERSVILLE. Built in 1869, the building remains in use today.

116

*This is a rather un-attractive picture of a pretty town.*

A BIRD'S-EYE VIEW OF SANDERSVILLE, LOOKING SOUTHWEST FROM THE SCHOOL.

East Side of Court House Square, Sandersville, Ga.

THE EAST SIDE OF THE COURT HOUSE SQUARE IN SANDERSVILLE, C. 1912. The general merchandise business of Wiley Harris and Son was located on the corner.

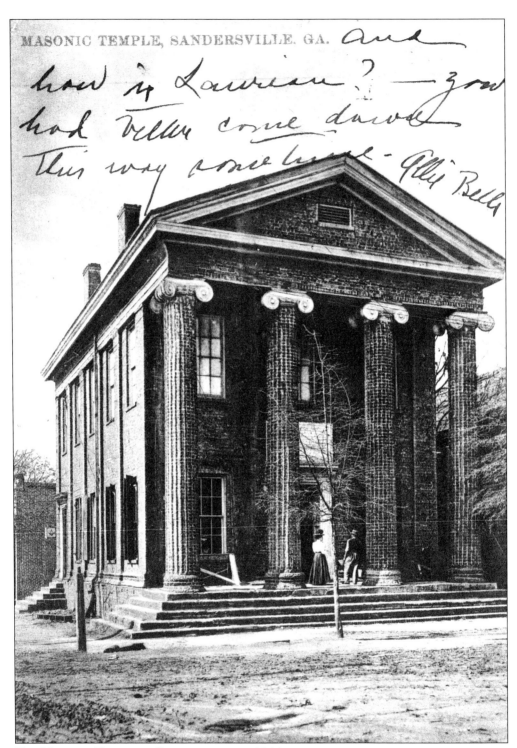

MASONIC TEMPLE, SANDERSVILLE. GA. *and how is Laurien? — you had better come down this way some time - Olli Bell*

THE MASONIC TEMPLE IN SANDERSVILLE, C. 1911.

RAWLINGS SANITARIUM IN SANDERSVILLE, OPERATED BY DR. WILLIAM RAWLINGS.

THE FIRST NATIONAL BANK OF SANDERSVILLE, C. 1912. In 1910, L.B. Holt was president and S.M. Hitchcock was cashier.

THE HOTEL SANTON IN SANDERSVILLE, C. 1911. The hotel was a beautiful Victorian-style structure.

THE HOTEL JULIDA IN SANDERSVILLE. This hotel was operated by Mrs. E.L. Pearson. The message on the card reads: "This is a very pretty hotel for such a small place as Sandersville. The Population is only about two thousand."

THE RESIDENCE OF W.A. McCARTY IN SANDERSVILLE.

THE RESIDENCE OF J.E. JOHNSON IN SANDERSVILLE.

The Residence of A.W. Evans in Sandersville.

The Public School Building in Sandersville, c. 1910.

122

THE METHODIST CHURCH IN SANDERSVILLE.

THE CHRISTIAN CHURCH IN SANDERSVILLE.

North Side Business District, Tennille, Ga.

THE NORTH SIDE OF THE BUSINESS DISTRICT IN TENNILLE, C. 1910. The Tennille Banking Company can be seen in the distance on the far right. The president of the bank was D.E. McMaster and J.H. Arnall was the cashier.

Pritchard Hotel, Tennille, Ga.

THE PRITCHARD HOTEL IN TENNILLE, OWNED BY H.L. PRITCHARD.

THE MAIN OFFICE OF THE WRIGHTSVILLE AND TENNILLE RAILROAD IN TENNILLE, 1910.

A BEAUTIFUL HOME ON THE CORNER OF SMITH AND ADAMS STREETS IN TENNILLE.

STUDENTS POSE IN FRONT OF THE TENNILLE INSTITUTE IN TENNILLE IN 1908.

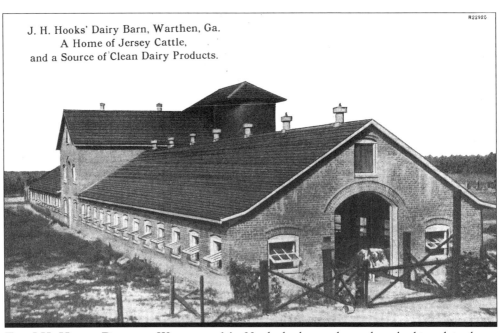

THE J.H. HOOKS DAIRY IN WARTHEN. Mr. Hooks had a modern, clean-looking dairy barn, where he milked Jersey cattle.

# BIBLIOGRAPHY

Anonymous. *1909–1910 Business and Professional Directory of the Cities and Towns of Georgia*. Atlanta, Georgia: Young and Company, 1910.

Jordan, Robert H. and J. Gregg Puster. *Courthouses in Georgia*. Editing and design by Patti Anderson and Mary Jackson. Norcross, Georgia: The Harrison Company, 1984.

Krackow, Kenneth K. *Georgia Place-Names*. Macon, Georgia: Winship Press, 1975.

McKenny, Frank M. *The Standing Army: History of Georgia's County Confederate Monuments*. Alpharetta, Georgia: W.H. Wolfe Associates, 1993.

Rozier, John. *The Houses of Hancock 1785–1865*. Decatur, Georgia: Auldfarran Books.

Winn, Les R. *Ghost Trains & Depots of Georgia (1833–1933)*. Chamblee, Georgia: Big Shanty Publishing Company, 1995.

# INDEX